Science Tools

USING CLOCKS AND STOPWATCHES

Lorijo Metz

PowerKiDS press.

New York

Dedicated to Barb and Joe Rush, who've dedicated so much time and love to me

Published in 2013 by The Rosen Publishing Group, Inc.
29 East 21st Street, New York, NY 10010

First Edition

Editor: Amelie von Zumbusch
Book Design: Kate Laczynski

Photo Credits: Cover RubberBall Productions/the Agency Collection/Getty Images; p. 4 Peter Dazeley/Photographer's Choice/Getty Images; p. 5 B.C. Moller/Taxi/Getty Images; p. 6 Jupiterimages/Brand X Pictures/Thinkstock; p. 7 Ty Allison/Photographer's Choice/Getty Images; pp. 8, 9 (bottom), 11 iStockphoto/Thinkstock; p. 9 (top) JGI/Jamie Grill/Blend Images/Getty Images; p. 10 tuulijumala/Shutterstock.com; p. 12 (goggles) Natalie V Guseva/Shutterstock.com; p. 12 (gloves) Nataliya Kuznetsova/Shutterstock.com; p. 12 (first aid kit) Oleksiy Mark/Shutterstock.com; p. 12 (wipes) Chas/Shutterstock.com; p. 13 blue jean images/Getty Images; p. 15 Felix Mizioznikov/Shutterstock.com; p. 16 Jupiterimages/Pixland/Thinkstock; p. 17 Gary Paul Lewis/Shutterstock.com; p. 18 © iStockphoto.com/Nathan Marx; p. 19 © iStockphoto.com/Tatiana Popova; p. 20 tubuceo/Shutterstock.com; p. 21 Will & Deni McIntyre/Photo Researchers/Getty Images; p. 22 © iStockphoto.com/Fengyuan Chang.

Library of Congress Cataloging-in-Publication Data

Metz, Lorijo.
 Using clocks and stopwatches / by Lorijo Metz. — 1st ed.
    p. cm. — (Science tools)
 Includes index.
 ISBN 978-1-4488-9689-9 (library binding) — ISBN 978-1-4488-9836-7 (pbk.) —
 ISBN 978-1-4488-9837-4 (6-pack)
 1. Time measurements—Juvenile literature. 2. Clocks and watches—Juvenile literature. I. Title.
 QB209.5.M48 2013
 681.1'13—dc23

                         2012033063

Manufactured in the United States of America

CPSIA Compliance Information: Batch #W13PK4: For Further Information contact Rosen Publishing, New York, New York at 1-800-237-9932

CONTENTS

What Are Clocks and Stopwatches?

Sometimes people complain about not having enough time. Other days, time feels like it passes very slowly. You can't see, touch, or hold time, but it is always passing. No matter how it seems, time always passes at the same speed. Clocks and stopwatches are tools that help everyone measure the passing of time the same way.

Do you have a watch? A watch is a clock that is small enough that people can wear it or carry it around with them.

Clocks break time into equal units to help us measure the passing of time. Stopwatches use these same units to measure time. While clocks measure time continuously, stopwatches measure time in events, like races, which have a beginning and an end.

You can't feel it, but Earth is always spinning. We call the time it takes Earth to make one full **rotation**, or turn, a day. The amount of time in one day is always the same. People break days into 24 equal units called hours. We divide these into 12 a.m. hours, followed by 12 p.m. hours.

When you are baking cookies, you need to be able to measure time in minutes.

If you are timing the runners in a race, you will need to measure time in seconds, or even parts of a second.

Clocks divide hours into smaller units called minutes. There are 60 minutes in 1 hour. Each minute is then divided into even smaller units called seconds. There are 60 seconds in a minute. That means that a day is 86,400 seconds long!

Analog and Digital Clocks

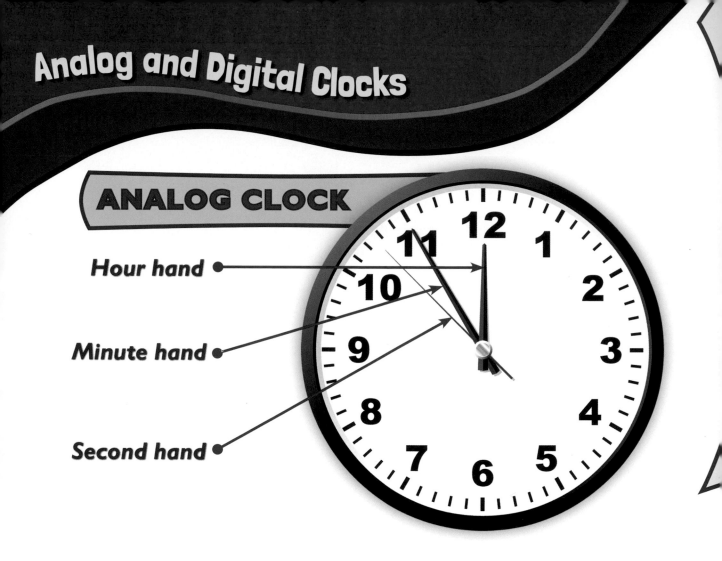

ANALOG CLOCK

Hour hand

Minute hand

Second hand

Analog clocks have faces with numbers for hours. They have dots or dashes to show minutes and seconds. Hands move around the clock pointing to the hours, minutes, and seconds. **Digital clocks** show time in numbers. The hour is to the left of a colon, while minutes are on the right.

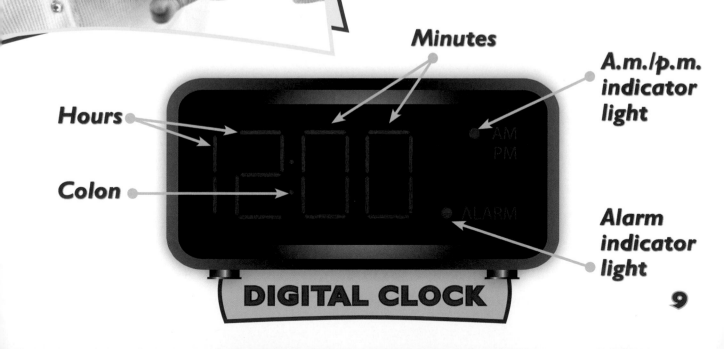

The hands of an analog clock can be hard to read exactly. Digital clocks that show seconds tend to be most accurate for timing.

A second colon may separate seconds to the right. Seconds may also be shown smaller.

To time something using a clock, note both the start time and the end time. Then subtract the start time from the end time to find how long the thing you were timing took.

Minutes

A.m./p.m. indicator light

Hours

AM
PM

Colon

ALARM

Alarm indicator light

DIGITAL CLOCK

9

Using a Stopwatch

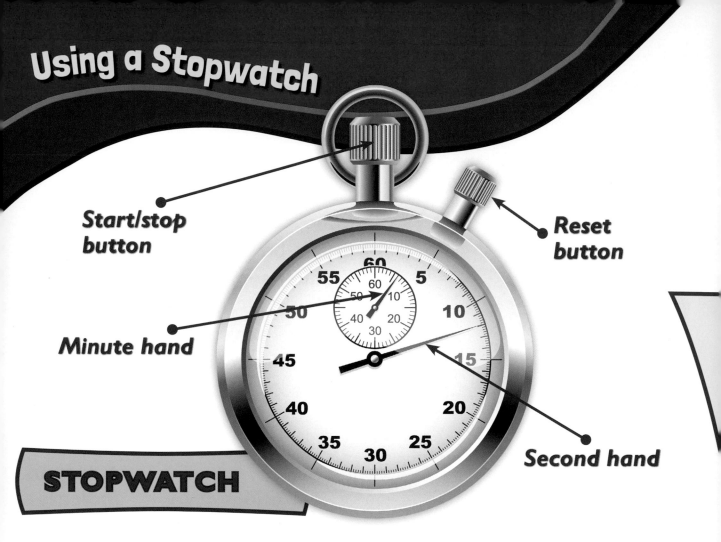

Start/stop button

Reset button

Minute hand

Second hand

60
55   5
60
50   10
50   40   20   10
30
45   15
40   20
35   25
30

STOPWATCH

Stopwatches have faces that display the time. Digital stopwatches display time in numbers. Analog stopwatches have hands that move around the face of the clock. Stopwatches usually have two buttons. One button is for starting and stopping the time. The other button resets the time back to zero.

To use a stopwatch, reset the time to zero. Push the start button when the thing you are timing begins. Push it again to stop timing. Record the time before you reset the stopwatch. Some stopwatches have a third button, called a **split button**. It lets you record two different ending times.

Some watches have stopwatches built into them.

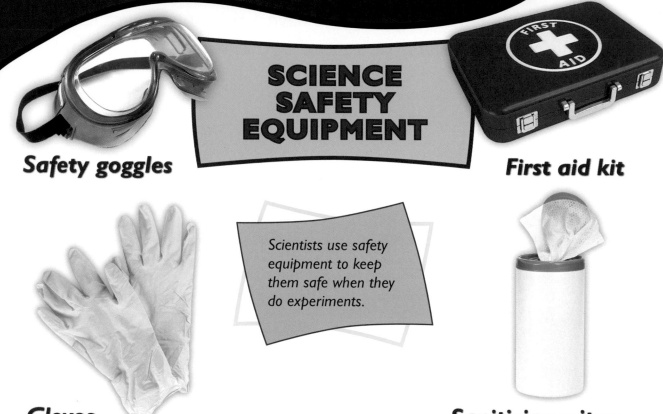

Safety goggles

SCIENCE SAFETY EQUIPMENT

First aid kit

Scientists use safety equipment to keep them safe when they do experiments.

Gloves

Sanitizing wipes

Scientists **observe**, or notice the world around them. They question how and why things work. Based on what they know, they form **hypotheses** to try to answer these questions. To test their hypotheses, they run **experiments**.

Scientists often repeat their experiments and average the results. This helps account for common mistakes, such as pushing a stopwatch button a tiny bit late.

Have you ever baked a batch of cookies too long and discovered they were burned? Just as time affects outcomes when baking, time is often an important **variable**, or changeable condition, in experiments. When conducting experiments that involve time, there are two important things to keep in mind. First, be sure to measure time accurately. Second, carefully **log** all starting times, ending times, and other measurements of time.

Our Sense of Time

Scientists are not sure how our brains keep track of time. They know that time seems to go faster when we are having fun and more slowly when we are bored. They know that some people are better judges of time than others.

Test your own sense of time. Have a friend shout "stop" when she thinks 2 minutes are up while you keep time with a clock or stopwatch. Record how many seconds off her guess was. Now have your friend keep track of time while you guess. Repeat the experiment several times. Compare results to see who has the best sense of time.

People often estimate seconds by counting out loud and saying "Mississippi" after each number. You can use a clock or stopwatch to test how accurate this method is.

15

How Long Does It Take?

People often want to know how much time something will take. How much time will it take to get there? How long will it take to bake? If you do something differently, will it take less time or more time?

Temperature can affect how much time something takes.

The type of pan you use is one variable that can change how long it takes something to bake.

Have you ever noticed whether icicles melt more quickly in the shade or in sunlight?

Try this experiment. Use two ice cubes of the same size. Place one in the sun and one in the shade. Measure the temperature in each spot with a thermometer. Time how long each ice cube takes to melt. Record your results. Can you think of anything else that affects how long it takes to do something?

Does your heart beat faster after exercise? You can find out by using a clock or stopwatch to measure your **pulse**, or heart rate. To find your pulse, tilt your head back. Find the long, bumpy area that runs down the center of your neck. Press down lightly next to that area with your middle and index fingers. The steady pounding that you feel is your pulse.

A watch is handy if you want to take your pulse after a run.

Set a stopwatch or watch a clock for 15 seconds. Count how many times your pulse beats during that time. Do this after sitting still and after running around for 5 minutes. Record your results each time. What do you notice?

You can also take your pulse by holding several fingers against the inside of your wrist.

Timing Experiments

Scientists have learned that most dolphins can hold their breath underwater for between 8 and 10 minutes.

Scientists measure many things with stopwatches and clocks. Some time how long animals can hold their breath underwater or how fast they run. Others also record how long eclipses last. Scientists time how fast certain kinds of soap kill **bacteria**. Bacteria are tiny things that can make us sick.

Scientists even use clocks and stopwatches to study how animals learn. For example, they time how quickly animals make it through a maze on different tries. A maze is a puzzle-like path with many twists and turns that lead in the wrong direction. The goal is to find the way out as fast as possible.

Mice and rats are commonly used in timed maze tests.

TIME TO EXPERIMENT

This experiment tests if sugar **dissolves**, or mixes into a liquid, faster in cold water or hot water. You will need:

1. 2 tablespoons sugar
2. Two beakers
3. A clock with a second hand or a stopwatch
4. A measuring cup
5. Hot water and cold water
6. A spoon
7. Paper and something to write with

Add 1 tablespoon sugar to each beaker. Add ½ cup cold water to one beaker. Stir with a spoon. Time how long the sugar takes to dissolve. Record the result. Add ½ cup hot water to the other beaker. Stir it, too. Time and record how long the sugar takes to dissolve. Compare your results.

GLOSSARY

analog clocks (A-nul-og KLOKS) Clocks that show time on faces.

bacteria (bak-TIR-ee-uh) Tiny living things that cannot be seen with the eye alone.

digital clocks (DIH-juh-tul KLOKS) Clocks that show time in numbers.

dissolves (dih-ZOLVZ) Breaks down.

experiments (ik-SPER-uh-ments) Actions or steps taken to learn more about something.

hypotheses (hy-PAH-theh-seez) Possible answers to problems.

log (LOG) To record day-to-day activities.

observe (ub-ZERV) To notice.

pulse (PULS) A single beat, sound, or throb.

rotation (roh-TAY-shun) One full spin of something.

split button (SPLIT BUH-tun) A button that freezes the time on a stopwatch while the watch keeps recording time so that it can be stopped to time a second thing.

temperature (TEM-pur-cher) How hot or cold something is.

variable (VER-ee-uh-bul) An element in an experiment that may be changed.

INDEX

WEBSITES

Due to the changing nature of Internet links, PowerKids Press has developed an online list of websites related to the subject of this book. This site is updated regularly. Please use this link to access the list:
www.powerkidslinks.com/scto/clock/